THE POWER OF YOUR WORDS

GARY KEESEE

The Power of Your Words
Copyright © 2022 by Gary Keesee.

All Scriptures quotations are taken from the New International Version® (NIV)® of the Holy Bible. Copyright © 1973, 1978, 1984, 2011 by Biblica, Inc.™ All rights reserved worldwide.

Printed in the United States of America. All rights reserved under International Copyright Law. Contents and/or cover may not be reproduced in whole or in part in any form without the express written consent of the Publisher.

ISBN: 978-1-958486-02-3

Published by Free Indeed Publishers.
Distributed by Faith Life Now.

Faith Life Now
P.O. Box 779
New Albany, OH 43054
1-(888)-391-LIFE

You can reach Faith Life Now Ministries on the Internet at www.faithlifenow.com.

CONTENTS

CHAPTER ONE : When Fear Speaks........................05

CHAPTER TWO: Desperate Answers........................13

CHAPTER THREE: The Sound of Thunder.................23

CHAPTER FOUR: Loose Lips Sink Ships....................33

CHAPTER FIVE: Fear Is a Lie..................................43

CHAPTER SIX: Stand Your Ground..........................53

CHAPTER SEVEN: Becoming God's Champion.........61

APPENDIX: Receive Your Inheritance Today..............73

CHAPTER ONE
WHEN FEAR SPEAKS

You are living in a day of extreme, intense, spiritual deception and conflict.

Spiritually, things are stirring. You probably know that. Now is not the time for you to be asleep spiritually. You need to hear the Holy Spirit on a daily basis. You need to let Him move you, warn you, and lead you. You don't want to be asleep. You need to walk by the Spirit in this day and hour.

You have an enemy. You need to understand that you are in spiritual warfare. You may not acknowledge it. You may not agree. But you are in warfare, and your survival in this warfare depends on your knowledge of how to handle it.

> *Be alert and of sober mind. Your enemy the devil prowls around like a roaring lion looking for someone to devour.*
> —1 Peter 5:8

Let's take a close look at this Scripture. The definition of "sober" means "to be circumspect," which means "to be careful to consider all circumstances and possible consequences, to be prudent, to be watching."[1]

So, you need to be aware of what's happening around you.

---

[1] https://www.merriam-webster.com

CHAPTER ONE: When Fear Speaks

If there was a lion outside your door that was trying to get to your family, how would that change your actions? Let's be honest: You would take some defensive actions and probably some offensive actions. You'd lock your doors. You might carry a side arm. You'd start to watch that lion and learn his patterns. You'd tell the kids to stay inside. It would change how you live. Isn't that right?

Knowing you have an enemy should change how you live as well, because your enemy is not just a guy wearing a red costume and carrying a pitchfork. Your enemy is evil, and he wants to take you out. So, you definitely need to be aware and alert.

What are you to be alert for? Deception and fear.

Here's the big problem with deception, and you may already know this. People that are deceived don't know they're deceived.

Similarly, what is the only antidote for deception? Truth. But people that are deceived think they have the truth.

So, it's vital that you have an absolute—and that absolute is the Word of God. It is the truth that you judge truth by. Not your feelings. Nothing else. The Word of God has to be your compass of what is truth in this day and hour, so you are able to recognize deception.

Remember, we are to be alert for deception and fear. Fear is an indicator of deception. Fear is not of God. Every promise from God is "Yes" and "Amen" (2 Corinthians 1:20). So, if there's fear in your life, it is an indicator that you're already deceived. You're already believing something that's not true. So if fear shows its head in your life, you need to attack it with truth.

If fear pops up in your life, you need to take a step back and realize, *Wait a minute. Right now, I don't have faith. I have fear. What does God say about this situation?*

You need to back up and capture that moment, and you need to deal with the fear before it deals with you.

You have to speak to fear when fear speaks to you. How does fear speak? In your thoughts—the thoughts that speak to you consistently. And unless you speak back, you're going to continually dig yourself into a hole that's hard to get out of. You need to speak back to fear louder than it is speaking to you—and you need to speak the truth of God's Word.

One time as a young pastor, I was facing some issues—and, of course, we all face issues—but I was praying and nothing was happening. So, I asked God, "Why aren't these things happening?

CHAPTER ONE: When Fear Speaks

Why aren't these other things fixed? Why are these things still hanging around?"

God gave me a dream. I saw a closet, and this closet was filled with shelving. But the shelves were empty. Everything in the closet was piled on the floor—big stacks of books and things. I heard the voice of the Lord say, "Speak to it."

So, in my dream, I said, "In the name of Jesus, go back where you were supposed to be." And everything on the floor went up on the shelves—*whoosh*—perfect, in order, neat, and at peace.

What was God trying to show me? "Gary, you've got to take authority here. You've got to speak to this situation. And until you do, it's not going to change."

He was teaching me how the Kingdom operates. In the Bible, Jesus never prayed to God to fix a problem. You'll never see Jesus ask God to cast a demon out or pray to the Father to heal someone. Jesus always operated in authority and spoke to the situation. He is our role model. This is how it works.

> *When they came to the crowd, a man approached Jesus and knelt before him. "Lord, have mercy on my son," he said. "He has seizures and is suffering greatly. He often falls into the fire or into the water.*

> *I brought him to your disciples, but they could not heal him."*
>
> *"You unbelieving and perverse generation," Jesus replied, "how long shall I stay with you? How long shall I put up with you? Bring the boy here to me." Jesus rebuked the demon, and it came out of the boy, and he was healed at that moment.*
>
> —Matthew 17:14-18

Jesus knew who He was. He understood the authority He had. He understood how to release that authority and how to handle the situation.

Unfortunately, so many believers today do not know how to handle it. When things don't align right—the Bible says it, but they're seeing something else happen—people make a decision to change their doctrine instead of asking God what went wrong.

God's Word never changes. If something is changing, it's not God's Word. You can always know that it's on your end. You've missed it someplace. It's something that short-circuited the Kingdom of God. That's why your knowledge of how the Kingdom operates is so important in warfare.

Paul was visiting a town one time, casting demons out and healing the sick, and some people there were impressed by the power of God being demonstrated, so they decided to try it for themselves.

> *Some Jews who went around driving out evil spirits tried to invoke the name of the Lord Jesus over those who were demon-possessed. They would say, "In the name of the Jesus whom Paul preaches, I command you to come out." Seven sons of Sceva, a Jewish chief priest, were doing this.*
>
> *One day the evil spirit answered them, "Jesus I know, and Paul I know about, but who are you?" Then the man who had the evil spirit jumped on them and overpowered them all. He gave them such a beating that they ran out of the house naked and bleeding.*
> —Acts 19:13-16

So, now let me ask you, "Who are you?" How well known is your name in hell? Evil spirits didn't want to mess with Paul. They knew about Paul. They knew Jesus. But who are you? What's your answer going to be?

If you don't know who you are in Christ—don't know your legal rights, the authority you stand in, or what truth is—then you won't have the right answer. You have to understand this. Ask yourself: How well known is my name in hell?

CHAPTER TWO
DESPERATE ANSWERS

You may know my story, how back in the days before I pastored I was very sick. I was dealing with some paralysis, panic attacks, and severe problems of fear. Looking back, I would say I was incapacitated by fear. I was desperate—really desperate—and desperate people find answers.

Fear is torment. Sickness is horrible. The doctors couldn't find out what was wrong with me. One of the doctors even said, "It's going to be interesting to see how this turns out." ("Thank you," I said. "I'm paying you for this?")

Then we began to hear about the Kingdom.

We heard about Benny Hinn. You may know that Benny Hinn has a worldwide healing ministry and holds crusades all over the United States. Perhaps you've seen him on video, praying at a conference for people. It's pretty amazing. We heard that Benny Hinn was going to be in Tulsa, Oklahoma, at the Mabee Center at Oral Roberts University, which is where we went to school, so we drove out there.

If you've watched any of his conferences, you've seen the people that are sick line up on one side of the platform for Benny to pray for them. He has the person helping him interview the person who is about to go up for prayer. This person will tell Benny, "Okay, this person has had this illness for so long," then they go up, and Benny prays for them.

CHAPTER TWO: Desperate Answers

So, I got in line, and when my turn came, Benny never asked what was wrong with me. The gentleman that calls out what was wrong with the other people never said a word.

When Benny saw me, instantly, he said, "Who are you?"

I said, "Gary Keesee."

"No, no," Benny said. "Who are you? A preacher? A minister? Who are you?"

He had picked up the office. I wasn't a pastor yet. I was called at age 19. But he picked up that anointing. He picked up my calling.

When he asked me that, I tried to figure out how to answer him. I didn't know what to say because I wasn't pastoring yet. We were beginning to teach people about how finances work, so I said I was an evangelist, because that's what we were doing then. We were teaching people how to get out of debt, which is good news.

When I said that, Benny just put his hand on me. If you've seen his anointing, you know it just knocks you right down. If you've seen Benny pray for people, you know sometimes he then says, "Get them back up," touches them again, and down they go again. He touched me four times—four times up and then four times on the ground.

He had them carry me off and lay me across the front row. The anointing was so strong that when Drenda came over and lightly touched me, she was out.

But when I got up from that anointing, I was puzzled because I still felt sick. I still felt horrible. I was confused. How could I still be sick under that kind of anointing? Remember, I was learning this stuff.

That night, I went to bed—still confused, still feeling that anointing on me, but still sick—and I had a dream. It was a very simple dream. It was just these words: "Therefore, when you pray, believe that you receive and you shall have it."

I woke up Drenda and told her about the dream and repeated the words: "Therefore I tell you, whatever you ask for in prayer, believe that you have received it, and it will be yours."

"Oh," she says, "that's Mark 11:24."

I said, "Oh, yeah. I know Mark 11:24."

But I really didn't. I had read Mark 11:24. I had heard Mark 11:24. But I didn't know it. As I thought about what the Lord was trying to tell me, I looked carefully at the Scripture and realized it says that *when* you pray, *believe* that you receive.

So, if you receive something at this moment, you

CHAPTER TWO: Desperate Answers

won't be looking for it in a future moment. You already have it. *Therefore, when you pray, believe that you have received and you shall have it.*

Oh, I saw it! I had been waiting for God to do something—but He was trying to get me to realize He's already done it. *Therefore, when you pray, believe that you receive.* That means you already have it! I told Drenda what I believed the Holy Spirit was telling me.

Now, at that time in my life, my body was all messed up. If I even smelled sugar or carbs, my body would go into a panic attack. So, I said, "Hey, let's go out and get some root beer!"

Because we had gone to school in Tulsa, we knew there was a root beer stand—Weber's Root Beer on Peoria Avenue—that had the absolute best root beer. So went down to Weber's. They have two sizes of root beer, served in those frosted mugs. I said, "Give me a big mug of root beer."

As you know, root beer is very sweet. I took that iced mug in my hand, I looked at Drenda, and I said, "I'm healed."

"I agree," she said. "You're healed."

I drank that whole thing.

It was the best tasting root beer I ever had in my life!

It was so good, I wanted a second one. I said, "Give me another big mug of root beer."

And I drank it down too.

I drank two mugs of root beer—no protein, no fiber, just sugar—and I felt fantastic! I've been healed of that ever since, praise God!

So, what happened? Why did I go home cloaked in that anointing but still feel sick? What was God trying to get me to understand?

Romans 10:10 says, "*It is with your heart that you believe and are justified.*"

What this Scripture means is that when you believe and you're in faith, it's legal for heaven to invade your life.

But then that verse goes on to say that with your mouth you confess unto salvation—that's when you release that anointing.

You see, I had the anointing over me, but I hadn't released it yet. I had the jurisdiction over my life. But God was trying to show me, "Gary, you have to agree with heaven that this is a finished work. You have to come into agreement. You know that I heal, but you have to come into agreement that you are healed now based on Mark 11:24."

So, as I sat there at that root beer stand and said, "I am healed"—*bam*—that's when the power of God was released in my life to bring the healing that took place.

Most Christians wait on God. They're waiting for God to do something. What I want to help you understand today is you have your part to play in how this thing operates.

If you've heard my story, you'll remember that after I was healed of those sugar swings and all the panic attacks, the spirit of fear kept trying to bother me.

Then one day, God spoke to me in my office. He said, "Listen, Gary, you are going to have to rebuke this thing. You're going to have to deal with this. You need to tell this thing to back up and back off—in the name of Jesus!"

And so that's what I did. I went into the restroom at my office complex, and I just had a little discussion—not with God, but with *it*.

I said, "In the name of Jesus, I bind you, you foul spirit of infirmity, you spirit of fear. This is not legal. I take my authority over you, and I command you to leave now, in the name of Jesus."

God said to me, "Pay no attention to your emotions. This is a legal issue."

I felt sick. The fear was still present. I felt those tormenting thoughts. It didn't leave right then. I went back to my office and sat down for about 20 minutes in my office chair, and, all of a sudden, the anointing came on me. I saw that demon leave—that black thing went right through the ceiling. And I was free! And I was excited! And I called Drenda and said, "Let's go get us some Chinese food! I am free!"

God showed me I had to rebuke that thing. I had to speak to it. God could not do that—*I* had to speak to that thing. I had to learn how the Kingdom operates. I had to learn who I was in Christ. I had to learn the authority that this gave me. I had to deal with it myself.

You have to learn the same thing for yourself. Stop looking for an oasis. The Bible says you're going to have tribulation. It's going to happen. Too many people are trying to escape the pressure or find a way out. Yes, God gives times for refreshing. But you're not here for the oasis. You're here to be in battle.

There may be times of confusion and problems and pressure. But there can also be peace in a storm. You have God's peace. You have His Spirit. You have the

CHAPTER TWO: Desperate Answers

anointing of God. You have the authority of God. But you are designed for battle. You are called to wade in among the serpents, set the captives free, lay hands on the sick, and command the demons to come out. You're not looking for an excuse to run *away* from those things—you're running in to find them!

CHAPTER THREE
THE SOUND OF THUNDER

A few years later, when I was facing some very difficult issues, I had a dream.

In this dream, I was standing on a hill with a sword in my hand. Below me, an entire army was spread out with their swords raised. And the word of the Lord—a voice in my dream—said, "Don't underestimate yourself, Gary!"

So, in that dream, I extended my sword and I screamed the word "Thor" as I ran down the hillside by myself toward this great army.

Later, I was talking with a friend who understands languages about that word "Thor." He told me that in mythology, Thor was the son of thunder—so this word had to do with thunder. (This was long before the various *The Avengers* movies were released.)

So, in my dream, God was telling me that I should not underestimate myself. "When the enemy sees you coming, Gary," He was telling me, "it sounds like thunder!"

In fact, God confirmed this dream later on as I was telling the congregation about it at our 2010 Provision Conference at Faith Life Church. I had written the dream in the front of my Bible. As I read the part where God says, "When the enemy sees you coming, Gary, it sounds like thunder," we heard a single, loud thunderclap!

CHAPTER THREE: The Sound of Thunder

On the live video recording that evening (6/26/10 at 7:53 p.m.), you can even hear me ask if that was actual thunder or just something my sound crew had done. That thunder was so special! And it was the only thunderclap that we heard that night. When I went outside, there was a single cloud above the church. It wasn't raining, but God was right on cue. He was saying, "Amen! You have the authority. Go deal with it."

You may be wondering what it means "to sound like thunder."

You may remember when the Centurion approached Jesus and told Him about his sick servant.

> *Jesus said to him, "Shall I come and heal him?"*
>
> *The Centurion replied, "Lord, I do not deserve to have you come under my roof. But just say the word, and my servant will be healed. For I myself am a man under authority, with soldiers under me. I tell this one, 'Go,' and he goes; and that one, 'Come,' and he comes. I say to my servant, 'Do this,' and he does it."*
>
> *When Jesus heard this, he was amazed... "Truly I tell you, I have not found anyone in Israel with such great faith!"*

> *Then Jesus said to the Centurion, "Go! Let it be done just as you believed it would." And his servant was healed at that moment.*
> —Matthew 8:7-10, 13

The Centurion was saying, "Look, when I talk to one of my guys under my authority, my voice doesn't sound like my voice. My voice sounds like Caesar's voice. And when I hear my commanding officer speak to me, I don't hear his voice—I hear Caesar's voice."

So, when you speak on behalf of the Lord—when you speak His Word—guess who you sound like? You sound like Jesus. Your voice has the same authority, the same twang, the same everything. The devil can't even tell you said it.

In fact, the Bible says, *"Submit yourselves then to God. Resist the devil, and he will flee from you"* (James 4:7). That word "flee" in the Greek means "to run in terror"—so when you speak, the devil will flee in terror because it sounds like the same authority God Himself has.

So, stop begging. Stop wishing Jesus would come and tell you how to deal with things. You already have everything you need.

Jesus doesn't need to show up in your bedroom to tell you what to do. He put the Spirit of God in you to be your Counselor. That's what the book of John says. He already gave you His authority, His Spirit, His Word, and the entire Kingdom. You already have it all.

But most Christians do not know how to dot the "i" and cross the "t." They don't know how to bring it to a close—how to bring it into the earthly realm.

Believe me, demons don't care how big God is in your life. They don't care that you go to church. But they do care if you learn who you are in Christ, if you know about the authority that Jesus gave you, and if you actually go out and advance the Kingdom into his territory.

The Bible teaches that you're like Joseph in the Old Testament.

Remember Joseph? He was accused of raping Potiphar's wife, and the sentence he received was "you-don't-ever-get-out." A Hebrew slave in an Egyptian prison? It was over for him.

But then Pharaoh had a dream, and Joseph interpreted it for him.

> *Then Pharaoh said to Joseph, "Since God has made all this known to you, there is no one so discerning and wise as you."*
> —Genesis 41:39

Notice that God made it known to Joseph. That's what the Holy Spirit does for us.

> *What no eye has seen, what no ear has heard, and what no human mind has conceived ... these are the things God has revealed to us by his Spirit.*
> —1 Corinthians 2:9-10

"There is no one so discerning and wise as you"? That's like us. We're ready for promotion here!

> *You shall be in charge of my palace, and all my people are to submit to your orders. Only with respect to the throne will I be greater than you.*
> —Genesis 41:40

The story of Joseph is a picture of what the church actually has now. Joseph is a type of Christ.

> *And God raised us up with Christ and seated us with him in the heavenly realms in Christ Jesus.*
> —Ephesians 2:6

So, where are you seated spiritually? On the right hand of the Father with Jesus. So, only the Father is above you—and you have all the same authority Jesus has.

CHAPTER THREE: The Sound of Thunder

Notice that Pharaoh told Joseph, "*all my people are to submit to your orders.*" Again, this is a picture of where you're at now. All of God's people—which are His angels—are here to back you up.

> *Are not all angels ministering spirits sent to serve those who will inherit salvation?*
> —Hebrews 1:14

There's more. "*So Pharaoh said to Joseph, 'I hereby put you in charge of the whole land of Egypt'*" (Genesis 41:41).

Jesus says to you, "*I will give you the keys of the Kingdom of heaven*" (Matthew 16:19).

Are you getting this yet? This is your territory. You have jurisdiction here. God gave you the jurisdiction and the authority to rule this place.

> *Then Pharaoh took his signet ring from his finger and put it on Joseph's finger.*
> —Genesis 41:42

Whenever a king made a decree, he stamped it with his signet ring. It represented his authority, so it made it law. When Pharaoh took his signet ring from his finger and put it on Joseph's finger, he was saying, "Joseph, you're in charge. You have my authority. What you say goes."

THE POWER OF YOUR WORDS

Then Pharaoh...

> ...dressed him in robes of fine linen and put a gold chain around his neck. He had him ride in a chariot as his second-in-command... Thus he put him in charge of the whole land of Egypt. Then Pharaoh said to Joseph, "I am Pharaoh, but without your word no one will lift hand or foot in all Egypt."
> —Genesis 41:42-44

Now you may be thinking, *Oh, I feel like I'm in prison right now. I wish that was my story! I wish someone would deliver me out of this situation. I wish I had all that authority and wealth.*

But you have been! You do! This is your story! Joseph's story is speaking prophetically about the church.

We see the exact same thing in the New Testament. In the parable of the lost son, the Prodigal Son returns home, and the father says to his servants,

> "Quick! Bring the best robe and put it on him. Put a ring on his finger and sandals on his feet. Bring the fattened calf and kill it. Let's have a feast and celebrate."
> —Luke 15:22-23

CHAPTER THREE: The Sound of Thunder

This is you! You're royalty now! The signet ring has been put on your finger. You have the authority of the estate of the King. You have sandals on your feet, which has the same meaning as a chariot for Joseph. You now have access to cover the entire territory. The fatted calf is the same thing as the necklace of gold. You have the prosperity of the entire estate.

Are you getting this now? This is you. Can you imagine Joseph having to beg for a meal? Of course not. He's in charge. He has the signet ring. What he says goes. In the same way, you have the authority to speak. You have been anointed and set in place to reign and rule in life.

Yet, probably most Christians—at least a large majority of them—do not know this. They spend their lives begging God to do something, and waiting on God to show up and fix their problem and heal their bodies. Think about it. When someone's sick, do you hear them talking to their body—or talking about their body to God?

The Bible says if you believe in your heart what God says, then you speak it and you believe what you speak, you shall have it.

> *Truly, I tell you, if anyone says to this mountain, "Go, throw yourself into the sea," and does not doubt in their heart but believes that what they say will happen, it will be done for them.*
> —Mark 11:23

Who is it that makes that happen? God's people—the angels—who are here to serve us. Naturally, we can't boss angels around (after all, they're the King's angels, and He gives them their assignments), but Jesus did say that if He had called, God would have sent more than twelve legions of angels to back Him up (Matthew 26:53).

CHAPTER FOUR
LOOSE LIPS SINK SHIPS

Satan knows that most people don't understand that they hold the keys to the Kingdom.

They're just waiting on God. They celebrate, cheer, clap their hands, and praise God—but they don't know that they have a part to play. They have the ring. They have the keys. But no one's ever taught them how to turn on the car or how to drive it. They know how to go to church, but they've never been taught that they are the church.

Drenda and I had a friend for a number of years who was always talking about her house. She was afraid of her house burning down. I thought, *This is weird. Her house is perfectly fine.* Yet she was always afraid that her house was going to burn down, and one day it did. It burned down. Sadly, our friend did not realize what she had been doing.

How does a king rule? He decrees. The Bible says you're seated in the heavenly realms. And so you speak your decree. Prayer by itself doesn't release the power of God. You have that jurisdiction.

In the early days of our church, one of our families had gathered for a big luncheon together and suddenly realized four-year-old Joel was missing from the table. So they went looking for him. Their home had an in-ground swimming pool—and they found Joel at the bottom of the pool, motionless. No one knew how long he had been there.

CHAPTER FOUR: Loose Lips Sink Ships

Joel's mom, Tina, and his cousin, Courtney, ran over to the pool. Tina cried out, "Call 911" before she dove into the pool and pulled him out. Joel was limp and unconscious.

But Courtney, who was 13, said, "No, Aunt Tina, we don't need to call 911. We have authority here. We need to pray." This 13-year-old had more revelation than most adults.

So, they begin to pray in the Spirit. When we pray in the Spirit, God is going to bring revelation about what to do. But nothing changed for Joel. He was still out.

So Tina, the mom, said again, "We've got to call 911." And this 13-year-old says, "No, we need to speak life to him." Then Courtney said, "In the name of Jesus, Joel, wake up!"

Joel immediately woke up and spit the water out, and he is fine today.

Notice that their prayer did not release the authority. But I believe that in that moment, as they prayed in the Spirit, the Holy Spirit nudged Courtney: "You have to finish this out now. You've acknowledged the authority. You have to cross the "t" and dot the "i." You have to speak it now and release it. You know it's there, but you just have to release it."

So many people don't know they have the signet ring. They don't know they're seated in heavenly places. They're still kind of scraping by, just hoping things work out. They're begging God. They're hoping God shows up.

But, my friend, He already showed up. This is the key. He's already done it. It's over. He already gave you the ring. You've already got it all.

Christians often think, "It's time to pray," which is fine. Prayer is good.

But they think speaking spiritual words is something they turn on and turn off. What they don't realize is that they constantly decree things. It's not that they just choose one day, "Now, I'm going to decree my freedom" or "I'm going to decree my healing."

No, they've already been talking about their body for a long time. They've been talking about a lot of things. They are already in position. They're already speaking and already decreeing—and they're already receiving what they've been decreeing.

This is why the Bible tells us our words are powerful.

> *When we put bits into the mouths of horses to make them obey us, we can turn the whole animal. Or take ships as an example. Although they are so large and are driven by*

CHAPTER FOUR: Loose Lips Sink Ships

> *strong winds, they are steered by a very small rudder wherever the pilot wants to go.*
> —James 3:3-4

I counsel a lot of shipwrecked people. They want to go one direction, but they end up somewhere else. How did this happen?

You are decreeing every day. You're either agreeing with fear and speaking it into your life, or you're agreeing with God and speaking it into your life. You already have the position. It's not like one day you decided just to jump in—"Okay, I'm going to decree now." No, you have been decreeing all along.

If people don't understand how this works, you know who they blame, don't you? They blame God. They tell me His Word doesn't work.

"According to the Word," they say, "I'm supposed to be over here. But instead, this is what happened."

"Listen," I tell them, "if you're shipwrecked, you need to check your compass."

Here's how God got my attention with this principle.

You may know I like to hunt. Years ago, God showed me how to hunt by faith and get deer. I sow my seed for a deer. After a while, I had gotten to the place where I could even name the sex of the deer.

This is important if you hunt deer, because you can only get one buck. That's the law. You can get five does or multiple deer, but the state of Ohio says you can only get one buck. This is to keep the herd in check.

But you can also get one button buck—that's a young buck with little horns. A button buck is counted as a doe because you can't see their horns at a distance, and that makes it hard to judge if it's a doe or a button buck.

On my property, I don't want to shoot the does. So when the season comes, I sow a seed for an eight-point buck and a button buck, because I hunt for meat.

I have years of experience with this. When I sow my seed, the deer shows up. So, one year I went out after I sowed my seed, and in 15 minutes, I had my eight-point buck. Just like clockwork, it works every time.

So, I went out about two weeks later to get my next buck, which should have been the button buck. I was in my tree stand, and I saw this beautiful eight-point buck about 200 or 300 yards away in the field, trotting right for me. He came into the woods and stood directly under my tree.

I was thinking, *Why are you here? I can't take you,*

CHAPTER FOUR: Loose Lips Sink Ships

because I already have my buck!

I was confused because I knew that it should have been a button buck. Why was the eight-point buck there? He stood motionless right below me for perhaps 30 seconds. Then I realized that he was on assignment. I put him there. He had to come. He could not move. I could almost hear his thoughts. *Make it quick, Gary, make it quick.*

So, I did then what I challenge you to do. When you think something is supposed to happen and something else happens, start praying in the Spirit and let God reveal to you what really happened.

I began to pray in the Spirit, and God said, "You need to go and check your seed. You sowed for this deer."

This confused me, so I got a copy of the check from the bank. On the memo line, I had written that I was releasing my faith for *"Two bucks, eight-point, one button buck."*

How many deer is that? In what order? I know this sounds crazy, but they always come in order. So, that's what happened—two bucks, eight-point, showed up. The button buck would be after that.

Drenda can testify that when I saw that, I began to holler and run around the house. I was so excited!

Not because I didn't get the deer, because it wasn't about the deer. It's about the Kingdom! That deer had no choice. He had to show up. He was on assignment. He stood there for 30 seconds, and then his tail flipped and he turned around and trotted right back exactly across the same field. He was probably thinking, *Whew, that was a close one.*

Clearly, I did not mean for that to happen. That's not what I wanted to happen. But that's what happened. Why? Because *I* put it in motion. *I decreed it.*

That really caught my attention. I wonder how many things I have said over the years that I did not want to see happen but have declared them into my life. In the Gospels, we see that Jesus cursed a fig tree and it died. And He spoke to Lazarus and he lived. Both with words.

In the same way, you have the authority, and you have the ring. So, you may be stamping documents you don't want to put into law.

You may have heard the expression, "Loose lips sink ships." That's from World War II. They had posters in the barracks and all over the place to remind the soldiers to keep their mouths shut. Don't put information in letters to home. Don't reveal information in phone calls. The enemy is looking for any information that will help them win the war. Loose lips sink ships.

CHAPTER FOUR: Loose Lips Sink Ships

That warning is for you too. Watch what you say. Knowing who you are in Christ and what God has given you is the key to life. You have the authority to decree which deer shows up. If your freezer is filled with venison—or if it isn't—that's your choice. Stop begging God or waiting on Him to do something when He has already given *you* the keys.

Don't merely *agree* with your circumstances. You must *decree* your circumstances!

CHAPTER FIVE

FEAR IS A LIE

Right now—at this very moment—your enemy is strategizing about how to get involved in your life. He wants to take you out. The Bible tells us to:

> *Be alert and of sober mind. Your enemy the devil prowls around like a roaring lion looking for someone to devour.*
> —1 Peter 5:8

So you're on alert. You're watching for him to stick his head up somewhere. What are you looking for? Deception and fear.

Why should you be alert for fear? Because once you detect fear in your life, you've already been deceived. Fear is a problem, because it indicates that there is deception in your heart.

Fear is not part of God's Kingdom. All the Bible promises are "Yes" and "Amen." You have God's authority. So if you pick up fear, that means you have to address that fear, deal with that deception, and replace it with confidence in God's Word. Remember, truth is the antidote for deception.

> *Do not conform to the pattern of this world, but be transformed by the renewing of your mind. Then you will be able to test and approve what God's will is—his good, pleasing and perfect will.*
> —Romans 12:2

CHAPTER FIVE: Fear Is a Lie

When you detect fear in your heart, what should you do? First, you must remember that the enemy has no authority. All he has is intimidation and fear. That's his normal mode of operation.

Second, you must recognize that you are in a battle. Being able to umpire your thoughts and understand whether something is of God or not is vital for your life. The Word of God helps you with this because it is "alive and active"—always discerning between soul and spirit, the spiritual and the fleshly (Hebrews 4:12).

Since you are in a battle with your enemy, Ephesians 6 is a very important Scripture to your life.

> *Finally, be strong in the Lord and in his mighty power. Put on the full armor of God, so that you can take your stand against the devil's schemes.*
> —Ephesians 6:10-11

The devil is always at work setting up schemes. He is devising schemes against you at this very moment. He is your enemy, and he is prowling around trying to catch you off guard.

> *For our struggle is not against flesh and blood, but against the rulers, against the authorities, against the powers of this dark world and against the spiritual forces of evil in the heavenly realms.*
> —Ephesians 6:12

Satan operates in a kingdom. Rulers are the high authorities of his kingdom, and he has various levels of authorities. Below them are the powers of this dark world and spiritual forces of evil in the heavenly realms, which are down here in this realm where you live.

> *Therefore put on the full armor of God, so that when the day of evil comes, you may be able to stand your ground, and after you have done everything, to stand. Stand firm then, with the belt of truth buckled around your waist, with the breastplate of righteousness in place, and with your feet fitted with the readiness that comes from the gospel of peace. In addition to all this, take up the shield of faith, with which you can extinguish all the flaming arrows of the evil one. Take the helmet of salvation and the sword of the Spirit, which is the word of God. And pray in the Spirit on all occasions with all kinds of prayers and requests. With this in mind, be alert and always keep on praying for all the Lord's people.*
> —Ephesians 6:13-18

You need the full armor of God, so that when evil comes against you, you will be able to stand your ground and keep your inheritance. What God says is yours is yours. You keep what the Bible says you can have.

CHAPTER FIVE: Fear Is a Lie

Fear wants to cause you to back off. The intent of fear is that you give up or back up, but you don't do that. You don't move. You take your stand against fear. You have the belt of truth buckled around your waist. You stand your ground.

In this Scripture, Paul is giving an analogy of the Roman armor, because that's where these people lived. They were under the control of Rome. So, they knew that the belt was buckled around the soldier's waist, and then the breastplate was set in place on that belt.

Paul is saying you have truth as your belt, and your righteousness is set in place on that belt of truth. If the Bible says you're righteous, that's the truth. You are righteous. It doesn't matter how you feel. This is a legal issue.

So, you need to understand how to fight with truth. When the enemy causes you to feel condemned, that is simply a feeling—but it is not truth. You need to pick up that truth and speak back to that lie.

This is your weaponry. It's your protection against the enemy's schemes to lie, steal, and destroy in your life. Your success in battle is based on truth. You need to become your own attorney and declare your legal standing in the enemy's face. You have to stand firm.

You have to be ready to move in battle *"with your feet fitted with the readiness that comes from the gospel of peace."* You will also need the *"shield of faith"* so that you can *"extinguish all the flaming arrows of the evil one."*

What are these flaming arrows of the evil one? They are the thoughts that come against your mind. This is vital to understand. The shield of faith is being fully persuaded that what God says is true. Your faith protects you by instantly extinguishing these thoughts that produce fear. A shield is held away from your body, so that means these thoughts don't even enter into your meditation or consciousness.

Something you need to understand is that if a thought does get past that faith shield—if there's no faith there and you pick up that meditation—this fear will begin to produce, just as faith does. Fear is simply perverted faith. When you pick it up and meditate on it, you incubate it—and it begins to produce in your life.

So, if a thought brings a pang of fear to you, you need to recognize that you're not in faith. There was no shield of faith in place to extinguish that thought. Because if it was extinguished, it would have no effect. That's why you need to be on alert for fear. It's an indicator that something is wrong.

The enemy is always going to push the fear button.

CHAPTER FIVE: Fear Is a Lie

He's going to try to gain access. He's going to send thoughts and circumstances your way, and you need to be aware of that and know how to handle it.

If fear arises in your heart due to a thought, you need to realize "Uh-oh, I'm vulnerable there! The enemy has picked up on that, and I need to guard myself. I need to get into the Word of God and make sure that the belt of truth is buckled. I need to get reestablished on the foundation of God's Word and make sure the breastplate of righteousness is in place. I need to get that shield of faith out there!"

The Word of God is vital to all this. Along with the shield of faith, we are also instructed to *"take the helmet of salvation and the sword of the Spirit, which is the word of God."* I believe both of these pieces of armor mean the Word of God.

The helmet of salvation is the Word God—it's thinking the thoughts of God, knowing the thoughts of God, renewing your mind, and being transformed by the thoughts of God. When you know God's good and perfect will for your life, that means you're rejecting everything that is the opposite of that. So, this is a helmet of safety—you're thinking the thoughts of God. You have the thoughts of God that act like an umpire in your thought life. And, as you know, everything in life begins with a thought.

The sword of the Spirit also refers to the Word of God. This is a little bit different, however, because the sword of the Spirit is in your mouth. It's what you say—the words that you speak.

> *And pray in the Spirit on all occasions with all kinds of prayers and requests. With this in mind, be alert and always keep on praying for all the Lord's people.*

Notice that praying in the Spirit brings the strategy of the battle.

So, let's review. All the pieces of the armor of God are protective, except for two. The first offensive piece of the armor is the helmet of salvation—thinking the thoughts of God—and the other is the sword of the Spirit, praying in the Spirit. You have to have a strategy, and praying in the Spirit brings you understanding of the strategy to catch the enemy off guard and to help you stay outside of his jurisdiction.

Because you have an enemy and you live in a battle, having the armor of God is fantastic. But you can't just read about this armor or hear about it in a sermon. You have to walk it out. You have to put the armor on, because as a member of the church, you are commanded to *"Go into all the world and preach the gospel to all creation"* (Mark 16:15).

The church spends too much time trying to protect itself from the devil, when the Bible says the gates of hell shall not prevail against the church (Matthew 16:18).

This means the church has the authority. The gates of hell are the enemy's defense, and there's nothing the devil can do to stop the authority of the Kingdom. Jesus has defeated Satan. So we're not supposed to be on the defense—we are command to "go" out into the world, casting out demons and laying hands on the sick. We have been given assignments for God!

CHAPTER SIX
STAND YOUR GROUND

In that dream where I was standing on a hill with a sword in my hand and a great army was below me with their swords raised, the Lord said, "Don't underestimate yourself, Gary!" So I raised my sword and shouted the word "Thor"—which I later learned means "Thunder"—and ran down the hill to battle that enemy army.

God was telling me that I should not underestimate the authority He gave me. "When the enemy sees you coming, Gary," He wanted me to know, "it sounds like thunder!"

> *To him who rides across the highest heavens,*
> *the ancient heavens, who*
> *thunders with mighty voice.*
> —Psalm 68:33

Every time you read about God's voice in the Bible, it describes it as being like thunder. So when you speak God's Word, the devil can't tell anything about it except that it's God's Word. And to the devil, that sounds like thunder.

So as I ran down that hill in my dream, God was showing me how to handle the difficult situation that I was going through at that time. The sword of the Spirit—the Word of God—was in my mouth. He was telling me, "Gary, you've got to get in there with the authority of My Word."

CHAPTER SIX: Stand Your Ground

You have a choice in situations like this. You can back up or you can go forward.

In my dream, I was running down the hill toward the problem, toward the conflict. That isn't always fun, but whenever you try to escape conflict, the enemy is just setting you up. Have you noticed that whenever you try to avoid conflict it, it often gets worse?

But when you run straight at the enemy with the authority of God's Word, it catches him off guard—and he runs away in terror! That's what the Bible says:

> *Resist the devil, and he will flee from you.*
> —James 4:7

With this in mind, let's consider the story of David and Goliath.

Goliath, as you know, was a professional warrior and over nine feet tall. David was a shepherd boy. King Saul had tried to outfit David with weapons and armor, but it was all too big for him. So David collected five smooth stones and put them in his shepherd's bag. Then he took his staff in one hand and his sling in the other and went down to the battlefield to confront the giant.

> Meanwhile, the Philistine, with his shield bearer in front of him, kept coming closer to David. He looked David over and saw that he was little more than a boy, glowing with health and handsome, and he despised him. He said to David, "Am I a dog, that you come at me with sticks?" And the Philistine cursed David by his gods. "Come here," he said, "and I'll give your flesh to the birds and the wild animals!"
> —1 Samuel 17:41-44

That's how Satan operates. He's going to try to intimidate you. He's going to talk about the problems you're facing. He's going to prophesy your end to you. He's going to tell you you're nothing, you have no power, and that it will end horribly for you.

But notice how David responded to Goliath's words. This is just what God was showing me in that dream.

> David said to the Philistine, "You come against me with sword and spear and javelin, but I come against you in the name of the Lord Almighty, the God of the armies of Israel, whom you have defied. This day the Lord will deliver you into my hands, and I'll strike you down and cut off your head. This very day I will give the carcasses of the Philistine army to the birds and the wild animals, and the whole world will know that there is a God in

CHAPTER SIX: Stand Your Ground

> *Israel. All those gathered here will know that it is not by sword or spear that the Lord saves; for the battle is the Lord's, and he will give all of you into our hands."*
> —1 Samuel 17:45-47

At this point, Goliath was moving closer to attack David—and David faced the same choice you do.

Your enemy is going to keep moving closer and closer. Fear always backs up. It gives up territory. It gives up authority.

So, what typically happens as the enemy moves closer? If an enemy is bigger and stronger, people back up. This is why Ephesians 6 says to "stand your ground." We don't back up. Satan is trying to intimidate you and pressure you to back up, but you have the authority!

> *Be strong in the Lord and in his mighty power.*
> —Ephesians 6:10

As the Philistine moved closer to attack, please notice what David did. This is vital for your future.

> *As the Philistine moved closer to attack him, David ran quickly toward the battle line to meet him. Reaching into his bag and taking out a stone, he slung it and struck the Philistine on the forehead. The stone sank*

> into his forehead, and he fell facedown on the ground.
>
> So David triumphed over the Philistine with a sling and a stone; without a sword in his hand he struck down the Philistine and killed him.
>
> David ran and stood over him. He took hold of the Philistine's sword and drew it from the sheath. After he killed him, he cut off his head with the sword.
> —1 Samuel 17:48-51

Notice what David did in this situation. He ran. How fast? Quickly. In which direction? Toward Goliath.

There are also other lessons in this story. What if David had been afraid and decided to march around Goliath for an hour or so, taunting him and playing with him while he tried to figure out how to move in on him? What would have happened?

Eventually, Goliath would have seen the sling in David's hand.

Goliath did see the staff. *"Am I a dog, that you come at me with sticks?"* But he didn't see the sling. The staff was a decoy. The sling was God's supernatural strategy. This is how you are to operate in your battles.

CHAPTER SIX: Stand Your Ground

If David would have waited, Goliath would've figured it out. We see this same strategy at work in the New Testament. Satan never would have killed Jesus if he had known the plan of God.

> *None of the rulers of this age understood it, for if they had, they would not have crucified the Lord of glory.*
> —1 Corinthians 2:8

Your offensive advantage is a supernatural strategy— operate quickly with intent, courage, and authority. If you hang back, you've already lost.

In our culture right now, we're lacking true heroes. Yes, there are heroes on the movie screen. We have the made-up ones. But this world needs real heroes, men and women who are not afraid of the conflict, who will take their authority, righteousness, and the Word of God and march into the fray to deal with the enemy. We are not called to sit in a church building and play patty-cake. God has called us to go out there and make a difference in people's lives.

> *When the Philistines saw that their hero was dead, they turned and ran.*
> —1 Samuel 17:51

When you step up in authority and righteousness— or righteous anger—and you begin to declare truth, the enemy runs! He is actually taken aback and retreats in a hurry.

God commands you to hold your ground. The devil needs to see you as fearless, and he'll stay away from your house. Your family needs to see you as fearless. Your coworkers, your company, your town needs to know you're fearless. They need to know that you're not one who is going to back down. They need to know you are the one who has the answer—supernatural strategies by the Holy Spirit—and you're going to march in there and help all of them.

I like to say there's actually only one kind of leader—a fearless one! The rest just have the title.

When you know that you're in charge and you have the authority, you will have peace. There will be no concern, no matter what is happening out there, no tension and no anxiousness. Remember, Jesus slept in a storm.

So, stop waiting for the battle to be over. That's why you received the Holy Spirit. That's why the Bible says you shall receive power when the Holy Spirit comes upon you—to lay hands on the sick, to cast out demons, to pray in the Spirit, and to discern how to move in situations. You will face battles in life—because God has called you to battles.

CHAPTER SEVEN
BECOMING GOD'S CHAMPION

If you want to reach your destiny and be all God has called you to be, there are three battles that you cannot back away from—three key battles that you must win.

We see this in the story of Moses.

Although Moses was born a Hebrew, he was raised in Egypt. As he grew older, he saw how his people were being abused, and eventually, he killed an Egyptian in anger. So Moses fled into the wilderness, where he made his home in Midian and was a shepherd for 40 years—and where God spoke to him in a burning bush.

> *The Lord said, "I have indeed seen the misery of my people in Egypt. I have heard them crying out because of their slave drivers, and I am concerned about their suffering. So I have come down to rescue them from the hand of the Egyptians and to bring them up out of that land into a good and spacious land, a land flowing with milk and honey."*
> —Exodus 3:7-8

In that moment, Moses is excited. He shouts for joy! God is going to do this awesome thing for the Hebrew people!

Then God says, "So now, go. I am sending ... *you*."

CHAPTER SEVEN: Becoming God's Champion

All of a sudden, the shouts of joy stop. "What? Me? Excuse me, God, aren't we talking about the biggest, mightiest army and military force on the planet?"

> *"So now, go. I am sending you to Pharaoh to bring my people the Israelites out of Egypt."*
>
> *But Moses said to God, "Who am I that I should go to Pharaoh and bring the Israelites out of Egypt?"*
>
> *And God said, "I will be with you.*
> —Exodus 3:10-12

At this point, Moses is still not convinced this is a good plan.

> *"What if they do not believe me or listen to me and say, 'The Lord did not appear to you?'"*
>
> *Then the Lord said to him, "What is that in your hand?"*
>
> *"A staff," he replied.*
>
> *The Lord said, "Throw it on the ground."*
>
> *Moses threw it on the ground and it became a snake, and he ran from it. Then the Lord said to him, "Reach out your hand and take it by*

> the tail." So Moses reached out and took hold of the snake and it turned back into a staff in his hand.
>
> —Exodus 4:1-4

When Moses throws his staff on the ground, it becomes a snake and he runs from it. So what does that tell you about the snake? It's a venomous snake. Moses knows it's dangerous, and he runs from it. But God says, "Pick it up by the tail."

If you know much about snakes, you know picking up a venomous snake by the tail is extremely dangerous. Not because they can reach up and grab your hand but because they're going to try to get to your leg.

Basically, God is saying to Moses, "Here's something you have to understand, Moses. If you can't trust me by picking up that snake, you'll never have the courage to face Pharaoh."

First, you have to win in the personal battles. We all have different battles

God is going to lead you to take on your personal battle—whatever it is—and you have to win that one. You have to see the victory. But you need to know that fear and authority do not exist at the same time. And where you're headed, you're going to need to know how authority operates.

CHAPTER SEVEN: Becoming God's Champion

So you have to deal with the personal battle on the inside first. This may be a battle that no one knows about—fear, lack of discipline, you name it. It could be an endless list. But before you can reach your destiny, you have to win this battle where no one knows your name.

David had to fight the bear and the lion before he fought Goliath. No one knew his name then. No one knew he was out there. No one even cared that he was out there. Of course, his father had entrusted him to take care of the sheep, and he had to be faithful to that trust. So, he looked to God to help him. David fought that bear and the lion, risked his life, proved himself faithful, and won those battles.

After you win the personal battles, you are beginning to learn about authority. You are learning how to exercise faith in those areas. This is when God is going to lead you into a public battle.

This is when David encountered Goliath.

What you may not know—and what most Christians don't realize—is that David was anointed to be king over Israel in 1 Samuel 16, but he didn't meet Goliath until 1 Samuel 17. This means David, the shepherd, had already been anointed to be king *before* he battled Goliath—but no one there knew it.

God Himself orchestrates the plan that will move

you toward your destiny. After you win the personal battles, God leads you into the public battles. Thousands of people saw David take Goliath out, and it wasn't long before we see that 400 men began following David and made him their leader (in 1 Samuel 22).

But David didn't get there by saying, "I'm your leader." He didn't have a sign out front that proclaimed "Leadership Class Here." He became their leader because he had evidence—his demonstrated leadership, courage, anointing, and confidence—and they followed him.

You need to understand that when it comes to your destiny, it will take other people. God does not call you by yourself. When you get to the place that God calls your destiny, there will be other people there. Whether it is your family, your employees, or whoever else the Lord may call, there are going to be people in your place of destiny besides you.

Like David, you have been anointed *before* your battle. If you've received the baptism of the Holy Spirit, you are already anointed. *"You will receive power when the Holy Spirit comes on you"* (Acts 1:8). People will begin to sense the anointing as God begins to move you in that direction, they will hear the vision that comes out of your mouth, and they will begin to see the evidence for themselves.

CHAPTER SEVEN: Becoming God's Champion

Back when Drenda and I were seriously in debt, barely paying our bills, people didn't want to hang around us. But when we got ahold of God's Word and began to change our lives, we got out of debt and began to have money, then people began to see the evidence of the Kingdom. As we talked more and more about the Kingdom, they found themselves drawn to the Kingdom.

We launched our company, we trained salesmen, and we had a monthly sales meeting. We had over 100 people there, but out of those 100 people, maybe only 30 people were actively making sales that month.

So, why did they all come? Because they liked to hear success stories. They enjoyed hearing and seeing what was happening. As they heard those stories, as they saw the evidence, they gained the courage to face their own personal battles.

Eventually, many of them began to step into public battles. They began to think, "Wait a minute. If it works for you, it'll work for me!" They began to step out past their comfort zones, and soon they began to have the same results they saw other people around them having.

So, as God continued to move and we were called to launch Faith Life Church in New Albany, Ohio, we found the people were already there. I'd already been teaching them every month for years, but we just hadn't called it a church. But just like those 400 guys in that cave who followed David, they saw the evidence for themselves.

Joshua was Moses's assistant, and when Moses died, Joshua was placed in charge. It was his job to take the people across the Jordan River into the land of promise. But there was just one problem. The Jordan River was at flood stage when God said, "Today is the day. Take them across."

But God told Joshua how to handle it: "Tell the priests to go first."

> *Now the Jordan is at flood stage all during harvest. Yet as soon as the priests who carried the ark reached the Jordan and their feet touched the water's edge, the water from upstream stopped flowing. It piled up in a heap a great distance away ... until the whole nation had completed the crossing on dry ground.*
> —Joshua 3:15-17

Does this remind you of another story? When God first brought Moses and the people out of Egypt, He led them to the Red Sea, where they were hemmed in by mountains on both sides with Pharaoh behind them.

CHAPTER SEVEN: Becoming God's Champion

He did this for two reasons. First, He wanted to eliminate the enemy. Pharaoh's army died when they tried to cross and the water came in. Second, God wanted to exalt Moses in their eyes as their leader, so they would trust him.

He did the same for Joshua after he led them across that river on dry ground.

> *That day the Lord exalted Joshua in the sight of all Israel; and they stood in awe of him all the days of his life, just as they had stood in awe of Moses.*
> —Joshua 4:14

This is the way God is going to set you in place. You will win the personal battle, and then you will win the public battle. People will see it and respect it, and they'll be drawn to that anointing and to your vision.

As great as the personal battle is to win—and it was a great victory for us to get out of debt and finally win against all the dysfunction, antidepressants, and demonic strongholds in our life—that victory wasn't the victory God was after for us.

Although I had a great public victory—people saw the evidence as we launched various companies, and they saw the anointing and the vision—both the personal and public victories were just hurdles

69

we needed to cross to get to the ultimate place of destiny God has for us to occupy.

When David saved Israel that day by killing Goliath, that wasn't the end of his story. It was just the beginning. King David went on to rule over Israel and to establish that great nation. He fought many battles, defeated all their enemies as they occupied the land, and led Israel to a place of peace where Solomon could build the Temple.

After the personal battles and the public battles, God led David to fight bigger battles—battles in the place of occupation.

The Bible tells us Goliath had brothers. When the spies were sent out to explore Canaan, they reported that there were walled cities and people that looked like giants. But the people knew they could trust David in the battles of occupation. They had already seen a giant go down.

It's the same for you. The battles in front of you are bigger than any of the battles you will face personally, and they will be bigger than any of the battles you will face publicly.

Eventually, like David, you will go into battles of occupation—and Satan despises giving up territory! So, God is going to put people around you to help

CHAPTER SEVEN: Becoming God's Champion

you take that territory. He is calling people to the vision He gives you.

Looking back, it's obvious that if Drenda and I had not stepped out, there would be no Faith Life Church. Likewise, if you don't step out, what future are you aborting? What is it that God has planned—not just for you but for the many—that will be delayed or lost if you don't step out?

Friend, there's one thing you need to keep in mind. Your destiny is not the road you're on—although many great things happen there—but it's the people that He's calling you to impact when you finally get to that place called destiny. Even now, those people are waiting for you to get there. Their freedom, their deliverance, and their future depends on you. That's your place of destiny.

APPENDIX

RECEIVE YOUR INHERITANCE TODAY

What we call the good life starts when you choose God.

Jesus came to give you the Kingdom. The Bible says that whoever calls upon the name of Jesus has the legal right to become a citizen of His great Kingdom and a member of His household.

As a son or daughter of the house, you have an inheritance. Since Jesus paid the price for you, you can receive the whole thing simply by asking.

Then your life becomes a matter of learning about your rights and how the Kingdom operates—and you begin to apply those laws and walk it out.

Today can be the day that you change direction. This can be the day that you say "Yes" to Jesus. All you do is simply acknowledge you need God like this in your life.

Pray this out loud:

> *Father, You said in the Bible that if I call on the name of Jesus, You will receive me, make me brand new on the inside, fill me with your Holy Spirit, and teach me how to live in Your Kingdom.*

APPENDIX: Receive Your Inheritance Today

I need that! So let it be recorded in heaven today that I now call on the name of Jesus to be my Lord and Savior. I receive Your salvation and all the goodness included with it, in Jesus's name. Amen.

ABOUT THE AUTHOR

Gary Keesee is a television host, author, international speaker, financial expert, successful entrepreneur, and pastor who has made it his mission to help people win in life, especially in the areas of faith, family, and finances.

After years of living in poverty, Gary and his wife, Drenda, discovered the principles of the Kingdom of God, and their lives were drastically changed. Together, under the direction of the Holy Spirit, they created several successful businesses and paid off all of their debt. Now, they spend their time declaring the Good News of the Kingdom of God around the world through Faith Life Now, their organization that exists to motivate, educate, and inspire people from all walks of life and backgrounds to pursue success, walk out their God-designed purposes, and leave positive spiritual and moral legacies for their families.

Faith Life Now produces two television programs—*Fixing the Money Thing* and *Drenda*—as well as practical resources, conferences, and speaking events around the world.

Gary is also the president and founder of Forward Financial Group and the founding pastor of Faith Life Church, which has campuses in New Albany and Powell, Ohio.

Gary and Drenda, their five adult children and their spouses, and their grandchildren all reside in Central Ohio.

For additional resources by both Gary and Drenda, visit faithlifenow.com.

Made in the USA
Middletown, DE
15 June 2024